"Ginette's devotional ___ ts a picture like how Jesus ___ .e-flect throughout the day ___ .uughout the week. They have blessed me at the right times, inviting me to take a pause and draw me closer to listen to what God is speaking to my heart. I suggest pairing these devotionals with pauses on a quiet morning before the chaos of the day floods in, and let the stillness of peace and comfort anchor our hearts."

Sarah Rocha, Women's Ministry Director
Mission:USA, Prison Ministry in Chicago

"*Hope Unhindered* offers short but soothing meditations that touch my heart and soul. I love how the vivid images stay with me for a long time and inspire me to pray and reflect more deeply."

Emily Grabatin, author of *Dare to Decide*

"There are some people with whom you want to lay your head down on their chest and feel safe. That's the feeling I get from Ginette when I read this devotional. I would want to nestle in my blankets and read it before bed because it's comforting. I can feel the Spirit involved in the writing, and I enjoyed the simplicity and the sweetness."

Val deVries, author of *The Worry/Free Challenge*

"As I read Ginette's devotionals, I appreciate how naturally poetic she is. The grace she writes with is so evident. It feels like heaven is writing through her and speaking directly to me to gain a higher perspective on my life's circumstances. Her love for God, passion for people and awe for nature seem to be her fingerprint on every carefully crafted devotional."

Jessica Theresa Ortiz, Survivor Care Advisor
Fight4Freedom

GINETTE ARMOOGAN

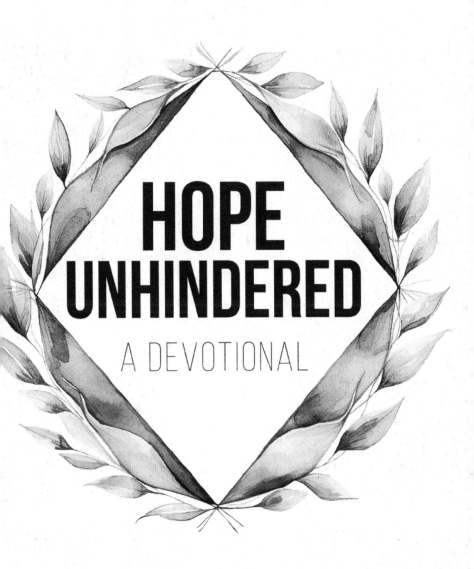

HOPE UNHINDERED

A DEVOTIONAL

40 DAYS OF ENCOURAGEMENT
FOR THE WEARY

This book is dedicated to
my precious gifts: *Caleb*, *Lauren* and *Nathan*.

May you always:
Keep your faith in God.
Passionately pursue the dreams He has given you—He made you on
purpose, for a purpose.
Maintain hopeful expectation—God is faithful.
Remember you are loved.

Contents

A Few Thoughts and a Gift

Dear Friend,

This life is a journey. It takes us from winding paths of magnificent mountain tops to dark valleys. At times, we may become weary, disoriented, discouraged, and think we are on our own.

In these pages, I've shared some lessons that I've learned over the years. They are reminders that God is with us on the road. It's my desire that wherever you find yourself along life's path, you will find encouragement.

Each devotional contains a hope-filled promise and an opportunity for reflection. You will find thought-provoking questions at the end of each reading. These serve as journal prompts that can also help guide your prayer time.

For additional encouragement, free scriptural affirmations are available to guide you in declaring truth and hope that come from God. You can download this gift at: www.LifeUnhindered.ca.

Let's walk together...

Ginette

Hope Unhindered in Creation

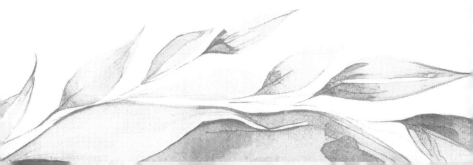

Out of the Darkness

After having a difficult week, I felt led to visit a small country church I had seen before on the highway, which offered a small prayer garden for visitors in the summer. In solitude, I sat on the small wooden bench, thankful to spend quiet time with the Lord and to bring Him the struggles that were weighing heavy on my heart.

As my eyes met with the ground, I couldn't help but notice the busy black ants that were scurrying around my feet. They were going in various directions on the patio stones - much like the racing thoughts in my head. Sometimes it can be so hard for me to just be still - but feeling determined, I continued to call out to God for help.

Changing my focus, I looked up at the tiny pool that I was facing. Poking up from the surface was a single water lily bud. I reflected on how they grow out of muddy waters to produce something beautiful. That single bud I was looking at may have gone through some dark waters on its way up to the surface. It was still closed, but it was only a matter of time before it would open into a lovely bloom. At that moment, I knew that I simply needed to be patient and wait. It was a reassuring ending to the garden visit that day.

"I waited patiently for the Lord; he turned to me and heard my cry. He lifted me out of the slimy pit, out of the mud and mire; he set my feet on a rock and gave me a firm place to stand. He put a new song in my mouth, a hymn of praise to

our God. Many will see and fear the Lord and put their trust in him."

Psalm 40:1-3 (NIV)

What an encouraging passage. The waiting will be worth it. God hears us and lifts us out of the darkness into the light. He gives us a secure foundation and a new anthem to sing. We can trade our struggles for a song, and the present mud for an anticipated miracle.

Promise of Hope

God brings us out of darkness and produces something beautiful.

Reflection

What are you waiting on God for?
What situations has He already brought you out of or transformed?

_____

_____

_____

_____

_____

_____

_____

_____

_____

_____

_____

_____

_____

_____

_____

_____

_____

_____

_____

_____

_____

_____

_____

_____

_____

_____

_____

2

Peace

I sat at my desk, my heart heavy from the hurt and disappointment I had been carrying. Resting my chin on my hands, I let out a long sigh. Suddenly my eyes landed on the serene peace lily blooming beside me. How interesting it was to be sitting next to peace, but not sitting in peace. Immediately, these words from scripture came to mind:

> "Peace I leave with you; my peace I give you. I do not give to you as the world gives. Do not let your hearts be troubled and do not be afraid."
>
> John 14:27 (NIV)

I knew that my own heart was indeed feeling troubled about many things. I was wrestling with feelings of fear and overwhelm. Yet, in this verse, Jesus was reminding me that He had peace available for me.

These meaningful words from Jesus were to bring comfort to his group of disciples at the Last Supper. Jesus had just predicted his betrayal, Peter's denial, and had told them he would be going away from them. The disciples were about to enter a very troubling time. Knowing this was to come, Jesus promised to leave them peace.

> How interesting it was to be sitting next to peace, but not sitting in peace.

The internationally recognized sign of surrender is the white peace flag. It's said that the white leaf-like spathe on the peace lily represents this well-known flag. The blooming plant's contrasting flower rising above a dark green base of leaves, was a reminder to me. Jesus had an offer for me. By surrendering my troubles to the Lord and letting go of fear, I could embrace the peace that Jesus gives.

PROMISE OF HOPE

Jesus gives us peace.

REFLECTION

What troubles are you carrying right now that need to be surrendered to the Lord?

3

Seasons of Change

As I survey my backyard during the dead of winter, the frozen landscape appears lifeless. The beautiful, vibrant flowers and foliage are now long gone. Apart from some empty branches, a thick blanket of snow is burying everything else.

At first glance, it may seem that everything is dead, but looks can be deceiving. My plantings are merely dormant. At just the right time, they will revive to soak up the cool spring rains and the warmth of the summer sun again.

> *"There is a time for everything, and a season for every activity under the heavens ... He has made everything beautiful in its time..."*
>
> Ecclesiastes 3:1, 11a (NIV)

Our lives can be like those seasonal garden flowers. Sometimes we feel vibrant and alive, with things around us growing and moving forward. Other moments may find us seemingly motionless or fruitless. Our dreams and desires are hiding under the weight of our circumstances. Barrenness is replacing the beauty that was once enjoyed.

> At first glance, it may seem that everything is dead, but looks can be deceiving.

Seasons change in both the natural world and in our lives. If you are experiencing a beautiful season in your life, enjoy it! Allow the momentum of expansion to propel you forward. However, if this season of your life is a long, difficult winter, be encouraged that it will one day change. Although we do not know how long the season may last—take heart, we will eventually emerge from this time.

Stay rooted in the Lord; we have a promise in our planting! Refreshing living water and the warmth of God's love brings renewal to our situations. In time, the barrenness in your life will blossom with beauty once again.

Promise of Hope

God exchanges barrenness with beauty.

Reflection

What does the season you are in look like?

_____

_____

_____

_____

_____

_____

_____

_____

_____

_____

_____

_____

_____

_____

_____

_____

_____

_____

_____

_____

_____

_____

_____

_____

_____

_____

4

Sunrise and Sunset

I love to stop and appreciate the breathtaking beauty found in both the sunrise and the sunset. The Creator's masterpiece painted across the sky invites me to look beyond what I see in the natural world.

The increasing light of sunrise illuminates the surrounding landscape in the morning. Likewise, God's spiritual light brings clarity to our own situations in life. As it shines, we begin to understand how God sees us: loved, wanted, and accepted.

> *"The steadfast love of the Lord never ceases; his mercies never come to an end; they are new every morning; great is your faithfulness."*
> Lamentations 3:22-23 (ESV)

The sunrise serves as a visual display of new beginnings. That first hint of light breaking through the darkness brings with it the promise of God's loving presence and faithfulness in our lives. As sure as the sun will rise in the morning, so is the certainty of God's love for us and His gifts of mercy that flow out of that love.

As with the sunrise, new beginnings are beautiful, but *a sunset is proof that endings can be beautiful too.* I think the most stunning sunsets are when the sky is awash with the fiery glow of amber hues which covers the space between heaven and earth.

"At sunset, the people brought to Jesus all who had various kinds of sickness, and laying his hands on each one, he healed them."

Luke 4:40 (NIV)

The people who came to Jesus may have started their life full of promise. But by the end of this recorded day, they were full of pain.

> Jesus is still with us, wanting to give us His gifts of mercy, healing, and loving care.

Yet, at sunset, they received provision for their sickness. That evening, Jesus met with *each* person who needed Him. By the end of the night, He had brought light into their dark circumstances.

This verse reminds us that it's not just in the sunrise moments of new beginnings that we can receive God's love, but also at the concluding sunset of something. Jesus is still with us, wanting to give us His gifts of mercy, healing, and loving care.

I don't know what place you find yourself today—whether it's one of promise, pain, or provision. But like those individuals who met Jesus at sunset, He sees you and loves you, and wants to meet with you too.

Promise of Hope

God extends mercy to us each day.

Reflection

What sunrise and sunset moments are you thankful for?

_____

_____

_____

_____

_____

_____

_____

_____

_____

_____

_____

_____

_____

_____

_____

_____

_____

_____

_____

_____

_____

_____

_____

_____

_____

_____

_____

_____

_____

5

The Greatness of God

> *"Your love, Lord, reaches to the heavens, your faithfulness to the skies. Your righteousness is like the highest mountains, your justice like the great deep. You, Lord, preserve both people and animals. How priceless is your unfailing love, O God! People take refuge in the shadow of your wings."*
>
> Psalm 36:5-7 (NIV)

In this passage, God's love and faithfulness are compared to the unending skies. His righteousness is likened to the massive mountains, and His justice to the vast oceans. With this, we get a more accurate picture of who and what is truly 'great' and deserves our attention.

Dwelling on the attributes of God diminishes the prominence of the giants we see in our lives. Things that are imposing or threatening cannot compare to the greatness of God.

Sometimes the cares and pressures in life can become all-encompassing and overwhelming. When this happens, it is important to take a step back. Refocusing on the Lord helps us to gain a better perspective of our situation.

The enormity of the cares and burdens we carry can make us lose sight of the reality of God's powerful presence.

We see the stressor, not the savior;
the situation, not the solution;
the demands, not the deliverer;
the responsibilities, not the rescuer;
the worries, not the wonder;
the mess, not the miracle;
the troubles, not the teacher;
the fears, not the Father.
In the busyness, emptiness, and longing,
the Lord is there for us.

> **Dwelling on the attributes of God diminishes the prominence of the giants we see in our lives.**

He beckons us to come closer to Him. In His presence, everything else becomes smaller again when compared to His greatness. In His presence, you will find your refuge.

Promise of Hope

Nothing can compare to the greatness of God and in Him we find refuge.

Reflection

What are some ways that you can find refuge in God's presence and maintain your focus on Him?

6

Storms

My first time on a cruise ship was quite enjoyable. The water was calm, and I was having a fun time until the vessel entered turbulent waters on the way home. Despite being on such a large boat, the few hours of rocking back and forth left me in a bit of a panic. I am a land-lover at heart who likes to look at the water, but not necessarily be *in* the water.

Even seasoned sailors can find themselves amid a raging storm. One minute you're enjoying a beautiful, peaceful ocean view, and next thing you know, you're in what feels like the fight of your life. Our life journey can be likened to a boat ride - sometimes it's smooth sailing, and other times you're battling an intense storm.

There is an expression that says, "A smooth sea never made a skilled sailor." Indeed, there is some truth in that statement. One cannot learn to navigate difficult situations successfully, without having experienced testing. So, what do we do with the challenges? How do we make it through the storms?

"Then we cried out, 'Lord, help us! Rescue us!' And he did! God stilled the storm, calmed the waves, and he hushed the hurricane winds to only a whisper. We were so relieved, so glad as he guided us safely to harbor in a quiet haven."

Psalm 107:28-30 (TPT)

Verse 28 reveals our answer: we are to cry out to God for help. When it seems like the waves are crashing over us and it feels like we might drown, we need to call out to the Lord who loves us. He alone has the power to speak peace into our situation and steer us to safety. Just as on the sea, storms are bound to come, but *how* we respond when they do come can help determine our destination. If you're in the middle of a storm, invite the Lord to be the compass that guides you. He will safely bring you to harbour in a quiet haven (v30).

PROMISE OF HOPE

God is our rescuer in the storms.

REFLECTION

What storm are you in or have you come out of?

_____

_____

_____

_____

_____

_____

_____

_____

_____

_____

_____

_____

_____

_____

_____

_____

_____

_____

_____

_____

_____

_____

_____

_____

_____

_____

7

Tenacious Thyme

O f the repertoire of spices used in the kitchen, thyme is one of the most widely used. This versatile staple seasons everything from meats, to soups, and everything between. The application for this herb seems endless.

Adding to this multipurpose plant's allure, is its proven health benefits. Its antibacterial, antiseptic and antimicrobial ability bolsters the thought that thyme heals everything!

Of all the ways thyme proves useful, the thing I admire most about it is its tenacity. Despite being a small plant, the roots of this gem will keep probing until it finds stable footing. It is a drought tolerant perennial that thrives in the sun's warmth and well-drained soil. The ancient world associated thyme with courage, bravery, and strength. Thyme certainly is tough stuff.

It's in the moments when I'm feeling small and insignificant, that I can relate to this little plant. In my search for significance, I long to grasp onto something secure and grow in a good environment.

> *"So then, just as you received Christ Jesus as Lord, continue to live your lives in him, rooted and built up in him, strengthened in the faith as you were taught, and overflowing with thankfulness."*
>
> Colossians 2:6-7 (NIV)

Like tenacious thyme, we can keep moving forward. Finding ourselves in the light of God's love allows us to bask in its warmth with our roots secure in Him. The journey may be difficult, but in the stretching and growing of your faith, you have shown courage, bravery and strength.

PROMISE OF HOPE

God will strengthen our faith as we are rooted in Him.

REFLECTION

How can you relate to tenacious thyme?

8

Harvest Season

W e know in Canada that autumn has arrived when the temperature takes a cooler dip. At this point, leaves begin turning colour and fall to the ground. There are many things that I wish I could bring into this new time of year - like the warmth of summer. Yet, there's always something that I look forward to - like wearing cozy sweaters and scarves. The changing of seasons always holds some excitement for me.

Autumn showcases pumpkin which is synonymous with October—hello Pumpkin Spice latte! But there is a natural order to what is grown, regardless of the time of year that it gets harvested. Typically, we plant seeds in the spring which get watered throughout the summer. Then, by the fall, produce ripens into a harvest for us.

No matter what you put effort into growing, it takes varying degrees of time to see the yield. Some crops grow quickly, while others take a long time to mature. It's similar to people that we invest time and effort in. When our work doesn't yield 'fruit' we may get discouraged. But, if the seed we were sowing and watering is the gospel, then we have a promise to stand on.

> *"As the rain and the snow come down from heaven, and do not return to it without watering the earth and making it bud and flourish, so that it yields seed for the sower and bread for the eater, so is my word that goes out from my*

mouth: It will not return to me empty, but will accomplish what I desire and achieve the purpose for which I sent it."

Isaiah 55:10-11 (NIV)

Don't become disheartened when you don't see the results in people that you are hoping for. Continue to be faithful until the next season comes. Keep sowing and waiting patiently for the harvest.

PROMISE OF HOPE

God's Word will accomplish its purpose.

REFLECTION

Where are you sowing or in whom are you investing?

9

Leaving the Nest

O ne spring I found myself gazing into my backyard garden more than usual. The ground was becoming green again. Dormant plantings like yellow tulips and a pink magnolia were coming back to life. Those of the feathered animal kingdom were also bringing forth their young.

There were little robin chicks nested on a ledge above my neighbour's front door. With weak wings, these birds could not go far and were making daily appearances in my backyard. The young robins rested in various locations: under a shrub, on the birdbath, on the arbour, or on the top of the fence. One day as I was about to water my plants, I noticed a little bird staring at me from beside my Rose of Sharon shrub. I laughed as I turned and moved to a different place to avoid drenching this tiny guy who had what I imagined to be a concerned look!

I would sometimes worry a bit, wondering if these little ones would be ok. Though the adult birds appeared to be out of sight, they would dutifully return to their fledglings. Then, the babies would simply open their mouths and receive their nourishment.

These birds reminded me of scripture, where Jesus says:

> *"Therefore I tell you, do not worry about your life, what you will eat or drink; or about your body, what you will wear. Is not life more than food, and the body more than clothes? Look at the birds of the air; they do not sow or reap or store*

away in barns, and yet your heavenly Father feeds them. Are
you not much more valuable than they? Can any one of you
by worrying add a single hour to your life?"

Matthew 6:25-27 (NIV)

Sometimes in our lives, we can find ourselves in a similar position as those little birds. We may be weak, in unfamiliar territory, or dependent on others for provision. Even if we have "left the nest" of safety, God has not left us. You are more valuable than the birds, and God's Word promises He will take care of us. He sees and loves you.

PROMISE OF HOPE

The Lord is watching over us and is our protector and provider.

REFLECTION

What are some ways God has protected and provided for you?

10

Seashore Promises

A fter a coastline visit, my husband brought home several beautiful seashells for me. Cradling these delicate little gifts in my hand, I thought about time on the shore spent with my family. There was always joy and excitement as we discovered new treasures.

One of my favourite things to do on any oceanside trip is to walk along the beach. Our family would always take advantage of the low tide to explore the exposed seabed. Our adventure would expand as the receding water revealed additional sand. We knew there was always something more for us to discover on our walk. Scuttling crabs, various shells, and even some stranded jellyfish captured our attention. We moved in eager expectation and attentive eyes, looking for something new in the sand.

The Lord spoke to Abraham about the sand on the seashore. It was a symbolic reference to the enormity of the things promised to come:

> *"I will surely bless you and make your descendants as numerous as the stars in the sky and as the sand on the seashore. Your descendants will take possession of the cities of their enemies, and through your offspring all nations on earth will be blessed, because you have obeyed me."*
>
> Genesis 22:17-18 (NIV)

It could have been a challenge for Abraham to believe these words. Abraham had only two sons and was already well advanced in years when he heard them spoken. Although he had gone through a difficult time of testing, his trust and faith in God held strong. Over time, God fulfilled His promises to Abraham.

Looking again at the shells in my hand, I thought about God's faithfulness in fulfilling all that He has said He will do. Just as the seashore contains innumerable grains of sand, the Lord will do far more. God's promises are bigger than our imagination. Like the retreating tide waters, we may even find other exciting hidden surprises as we walk in faith. Be patient my friend, new things are coming!

PROMISE OF HOPE

God's promises are bigger than our imagination.

REFLECTION

What is a recent discovery you have made in your walk with God?

Hope Unhindered in People

11

Disappointment

E veryone feels disappointed in people at some point. We're only human; it's to be expected. The bigger question is: have you ever felt disappointed or let down by God? I'm sure there may be individuals who have not experienced it, and others who would rather deny it. Yet, feeling disappointed in God can and does happen.

Disappointment is difficult. Answers are not always forthcoming. Even David, who was dubbed, 'a man after God's own heart' struggled with this at times.

> *"How long, Lord? Will you forget me forever? How long will you hide your face from me? How long must I wrestle with my thoughts and day after day have sorrow in my heart? How long will my enemy triumph over me? Look on me and answer, Lord my God. Give light to my eyes, or I will sleep in death, and my enemy will say, 'I have overcome him,' and my foes will rejoice when I fall."*
>
> Psalm 13:1-4 (NIV)

David's repeated question, "How long?" can conjure up many thoughts and feelings. It's an inquiry that we're all too familiar with:

How long until that significant need is met?

> **It's ok to feel disappointed and voice our thoughts to God.**

How long until things turn around and start going right in my life?

How long until that lifelong dream is achieved?

How long until that ongoing prayer request is answered?

How long...? How long??

It's okay to feel disappointed and voice our thoughts to God. David asked the questions, but that's not all he did. It's so interesting to note that there is no recorded response from God. Yet, verses 5-6 reveal David's own call to action:

> *"But I trust in your unfailing love; my heart rejoices in your salvation. I will sing the Lord's praise, for he has been good to me."*

David serves as an example of how to *praise through the pain*. This is something to remember in our own moments of disappointment when God seems to be silent. David focused on what he could do, and what he knew about God. Though David's life circumstances seemed bad at that moment, he remembered that God was still good.

Promise of Hope

God's goodness and love are constant.

Reflection

What does it look like to trust in God's unfailing love when life gives you heartbreak?

12

A Messy Masterpiece

H er life had become punctuated by shame and disgrace. This Samaritan woman lived condemned and ostracized by the culture. Hers was a history of failed relationships and questionable 'choices.' As a result, freedom from her painful situation seemed unattainable.

The routine task of gathering water was a continuous reminder of her circumstances and the rejection she experienced. She was alone in the heat of the noonday sun. Going at a time when the temperatures were cooler, would leave her to face shunning by other women. There seemed to be no resolution in sight.

When the 'woman at the well' encountered Jesus, the trajectory of her life changed. With just one divine conversation there was *transformation out of the turmoil,* and *commissioning out of the chaos.*

> With just one divine conversation there was transformation out of the turmoil, and commissioning out of the chaos.

Early church historians identified her baptismal name to be Photina (Photini). After joyfully leaving the well on that life-altering day, she became the first female evangelist. Though once avoidant of people, Photina became bold with others. She went around telling everyone about the one who knew everything about her and still loved her. Countless lives changed because of Photina's fearless testimony. She had been transformed into a confident woman driven with purpose.

> *"Many of the Samaritans from that town believed in him because of the woman's testimony, 'He told me everything I ever did.'"*

John 4:39 (NIV)

What a difference Jesus makes. The things in this life that we search for and cling to will fail to quench our thirst. When we exchange those to embrace the only One who can truly satisfy our deepest needs, we are changed. No matter how messy the pages of our life may seem, Jesus can transform it into a masterpiece... a compelling story worth sharing to all!

PROMISE OF HOPE

Jesus brings transformation out of turmoil and commissioning out of chaos.

REFLECTION

What do you need to exchange to fully embrace what Jesus is offering you?

_____

_____

_____

_____

_____

_____

_____

_____

_____

_____

_____

_____

_____

_____

_____

_____

_____

_____

_____

_____

_____

_____

_____

_____

_____

_____

_____

13

God Sees You

> *"The angel of the Lord came and sat down under the oak in Ophrah that belonged to Joash the Abiezrite, where his son Gideon was threshing wheat in a winepress to keep it from the Midianites. When the angel of the Lord appeared to Gideon, he said, 'The Lord is with you, mighty warrior.'"*
>
> Judges 6:11-12 (NIV)

The normal and best place for threshing wheat was out in the open where the wind could carry away the chaff. However, Gideon is hiding under a tree while doing his job in a winepress. He was fearful of the Midianites, and so, he chose to conduct his work unseen, in a much more difficult place. Gideon's life was marked by insecurity and fearfulness. When the angel of the Lord showed up, he called Gideon a "mighty warrior." The reality though, was that Gideon was quite the opposite of that. In fact, he didn't even acknowledge the title that had been given to him when he responded to the angel of the Lord.

I wonder how often we let fear and circumstances dictate our actions. Like Gideon, our effectiveness lessens when we attempt to retreat or hide. It's amazing that God sees what we do not, and He finds us in our brokenness and gives us a new title such as these:

God's child (Galatians 3:26)

Jesus' friend (John 15:15)

A chosen people, a holy nation, a royal priesthood (1 Peter 2:9)

God's messenger to the world (Acts 1:8)

Disciple-maker (Matthew 28:19)

Salt of the earth (Matthew 5:13)

Light of the world (Matthew 5:14)

Christ's ambassadors (2 Corinthians 5:20)

Knowing who God says we are gives us the courage to do what He wants us to do. Gideon didn't see himself as a mighty warrior, but God knew what he would become. Whether or not you realize it, God has already decreed who *you* are and knows what you will become.

PROMISE OF HOPE

God sees our future and who we are purposed to become.

REFLECTION

How do you see yourself? How does it line up with what God says about you?

_____

_____

_____

_____

_____

_____

_____

_____

_____

_____

_____

_____

_____

_____

_____

_____

_____

_____

_____

_____

_____

_____

_____

_____

_____

_____

_____

_____

14

Barrenness to Fullness

The disappointment from unfulfilled dreams and desires still weighed heavy on Hannah's heart and mind. To add insult to injury, she was cruelly taunted because of her situation. Expressing her pain only met with misunderstanding from both her husband and the spiritual leader in her life. The heartache of infertility pushed Hannah to cry out to God for a son. As a result, the place of barrenness became watered by her tears and transformed to a place of fullness. The Lord answered her prayer and Hannah gave birth to Samuel. Her child became one of the Old Testament prophets and the one who anointed both King Saul and King David. Through Hannah's pain God produced a prophet. Through this prophet, God produced kingships.

Infertility is not exclusive to the ability to bear children. Perhaps there are other areas in your life that seem barren. Things like friendships, workplace, family life and personal health are all areas that we can experience emptiness or loss. Like Hannah, you may also feel misunderstood, mistreated, or even forgotten. Hannah only asked to have a son, but God had much bigger plans that extended beyond her family. Samuel was not only a blessing to his mom; he was a gift to the nation of Israel.

The Lord wants you to bear fruit not only for yourself, but to have fruit that impacts the world around you. Continue to cry out to God over those empty, barren places. Remember, that He may have more in mind for you then you are currently asking for.

> **"So in the course of time Hannah became pregnant and gave birth to a son. She named him Samuel, saying, 'Because I asked the Lord for him.'"**
>
> 1 Samuel 1:20 (NIV)

PROMISE OF HOPE

God hears our prayers and has a plan.

REFLECTION

What fruit might God be wanting to produce?

_____

_____

_____

_____

_____

_____

_____

_____

_____

_____

_____

_____

_____

_____

_____

_____

_____

_____

_____

_____

_____

_____

_____

_____

_____

_____

_____

_____

_____

15

Wandering Warrior

D avid had been described as a brave and celebrated fighter until he lost favour with King Saul. Indeed, he was such a warrior, but it's interesting how seasons in life change. This can temporarily alter the way we act and how others view us. In David's case, things altered drastically. *A warrior became a wanderer.*

While David was fleeing from Saul, he stopped to grab some 'supplies' from Ahimelech, the priest. He left with some consecrated bread and the sword of the Philistine giant Goliath. David had originally taken the weapon in a brave moment of victory—it had been a battle that he ran *to*. But now, David was running *away* from his enemy. *A fighter became a fugitive.*

Ironically, David took Goliath's sword with him to Philistine. This is where it had initially come from, and where David thought he would be safer than in his own land. However, the servants of the Philistine king recognized the fugitive. David avoided capture by pretending to be mentally ill. He avoided harm when the king sent him away on account of his behaviour. Up until this point, David had been bold and courageous. Yet, in this moment, he found himself full of fear, in enemy territory, and looking for a way to escape. *The brave became bewildering.*

This incident inspired David to write this powerful testimony to what happened:

"I sought the Lord, and he answered me; he delivered me from all my fears. Those who look to him are radiant; their faces are never covered with shame. This poor man called, and the Lord heard him; he saved him out of all his troubles. The angel of the Lord encamps around those who fear him, and he delivers them."

Psalm 34: 4-7 (NIV)

David may have been in the enemy's camp, but the Lord was encamped around David. At times, it may seem like trouble is all around you, and you are in a season of wandering or bewilderment. Remember that the Lord is surrounding you as He encircled David. Keep pursuing God and watch what He will do. You are still a warrior and God is still delivering His people from trouble.

> **The Lord is surrounding you as He encircled David.**

PROMISE OF HOPE

The Lord is our deliverer.

REFLECTION

What season do you find yourself in? What might God want you to remember during this time?

16

Hope

M ost of us have things we are hoping for. Our hopes may be simple: like getting into the shortest line at the grocery store or cruising through all green lights on the road when we're running late. Other hopes are big: like witnessing a family member come to faith or seeing the end to an unjust societal evil.

At times, our hope may be misplaced, like with Saul during the early church period. He was breathing out murderous threats and was hoping to arrest Christians. This misplaced hope transformed into an overflowing, life-giving hope found in Jesus. After his conversion (Acts 9), Saul became known as Paul. Later, he went on to write thirteen out of the twenty-seven books of the New Testament. He travelled on three missionary trips where he preached about Jesus. While in the city of Corinth on his third trip, he authored the book of Romans—his letter to the Roman Christians.

> *"May the God of hope fill you with all joy and peace as you trust in him, so that you may overflow with hope by the power of the Holy Spirit."*
>
> Romans 15:13 (NIV)

How incredible! This man, who was once full of rage and bent on violence towards Christians, became motivated by love. Paul at one time thought he was working on behalf of a god of vengeance but was now telling others about the God of hope. According to verse thirteen, when we trust God, He fills us with joy and peace. The overflow of that is hope. In God's economy, it's a two-for-one deal, plus a bonus!

It's this hope that spurred Paul to passionately share the gospel. His actions have also resulted in a global impact. Placing our trust in the true source of hope will not only change our lives, but it can also change the world.

Promise of Hope

God wants to fill us with joy, peace, and hope.

Reflection

What are you hoping for?

17

Promises in the Desert

I named my firstborn after the Caleb found in Joshua 14. It's always been my prayer that his life would bear similarities to that of his namesake—and it's why this story is especially meaningful to me.

When Moses sent twelve spies to check out the promised land of Canaan, only Caleb and Joshua came back with a good report. Here, tucked in the pages of scripture, we find important life lessons.

Caleb was FEARLESS as a spy in the land of Canaan. He saw a victorious adventure awaiting Israel when he kept his focus on God and His promises. Others only saw obstacles and defeat looming in the future.

> How our circumstances or situations look like will depend upon the lens we choose to view them by.

How our circumstances or situations look will depend upon the lens we choose to view them by. *Be brave.*

Caleb was FERVENT. When the Israelites considered returning to Egypt, Caleb and Joshua tore their clothes in dismay. They passionately encouraged the crowd to enter the promised land rather than continue in their fear and rebellion. Our passions should be in alignment with our obedience to God, not with the crowd. *Be willing to stand out.*

Caleb was a wholehearted FOLLOWER of God and so the Lord declared that He would bring him to the promised land and his descendants would inherit it. This hope was deferred for 40 years while a disobedient generation died off wandering in the desert, but Caleb remained committed. Detours or roadblocks in life can happen, but God's promises to us remain. *Be patient.*

Caleb was FAITHFUL to God's intended plan. Even at 85 years old, Caleb was still strong and determined when it came time to fight for his inherited part of the promised land. God may have promised us something, but sometimes we still need to fight to take possession of it. *Be a warrior.*

> **"But because my servant Caleb has a different spirit and follows me wholeheartedly, I will bring him into the land he went to, and his descendants will inherit it."**
>
> Numbers 14:24 (NIV)

You may find yourself the odd one out as you determine to walk in obedience to the Lord. Perhaps you feel as if you're in a holding pattern while time marches on. Maybe you are contending in prayer for an unfulfilled promise. Wherever you find yourself today, be faithful in the desert, as you wait for God's promises to be fulfilled in your life.

PROMISE OF HOPE

God honours our faithfulness.

REFLECTION

What lessons from Caleb's life do you relate to or feel challenged by?

_____

_____

_____

_____

_____

_____

_____

_____

_____

_____

_____

_____

_____

_____

_____

_____

_____

_____

_____

_____

_____

_____

_____

_____

_____

_____

_____

_____

18

Taking a Risk

W ild rumors had been circulating in the city causing all who heard them to melt in fear. Could these riveting tales of God-given military victories and supernatural events really be true?

Rahab clearly believed the stories. She endangered her own life by hiding the Israelite spies who came to Jericho and provided safe passage for them to leave her city. In exchange for her actions, her and her family's lives would be spared when the spies would return with their army. It was a huge gamble, but Jericho was going down (literally), and she opted to align herself with God's chosen people. Rahab was ready to trade her familiar, but doomed life for the hope of something new and different.

When God calls us to a place that is risky, He is setting us up to see his hand at work. Rahab maintained an unwavering commitment and allegiance during a distressing time of uncertainty. This resulted in the protection and salvation of her and her family.

> *"But Joshua spared Rahab the prostitute, with her family and all who belonged to her, because she hid the men Joshua had sent as spies to Jericho—and she lives among the Israelites to this day."*
>
> Joshua 6:25 (NIV)

Obedience in our present vulnerability can unlock our future destiny. After the fall of Jericho, Rahab's extraordinary story was added to

Israel's rich history. It marked the beginning of the nation's entrance into their promised land. It was also the start of a new life for Rahab. Despite coming from an enemy nation and having a dark past, she had the honour of being included in the genealogy of Jesus Christ. The details of this remarkable story were intentionally included in the Bible. This bears witness to the fact that our past does not determine our potential.

PROMISE OF HOPE

God sees our potential.

REFLECTION

What does your obedience to God look like in the areas where you feel vulnerable?

Hope Unhindered as God's Child

19

Faithful

One weekend, while visiting my friend at her basement apartment, I kept hearing a familiar song throughout the days we spent there. The words of the traditional Christmas carol, "O come, all ye faithful", drifted down from the living space above. The elderly singer had formerly been in a motorcycle gang, but Jesus changed his life. He became a pastor and served for many decades in ministry. Although Alzheimer's had begun its deterioration on his brain, this sweet man continues to 'come and adore' the Lord. It wasn't yet the Christmas season, but those words gave me a fresh appreciation for the meaning found in this beloved classic.

The song lyrics reminded me that even when our physical or mental strength fade, we are still God's children—victorious and faithful. It's not our own efforts that give us worth, but our identity in Christ. I love it when God unexpectedly uses the voice of others to speak His words of truth into my life.

Although the man I heard singing is no longer pastoring, God is still using him to minister. Lack of position or title does not negate our role in the Kingdom of God.

Regardless of the day on the calendar, any time of the year is the right time for what scripture encourages us to do:

"Come, let us sing for joy to the Lord; let us shout aloud to the Rock of our salvation. Let us come before him with thanksgiving and extol him with music and song."

Psalm 95:1-2 (NIV)

Promise of Hope

God is our salvation, and we are his children.

Reflection

How has God been faithful in your life?

20

Wounded to Warrior

I credit growing up in a military family, for why I naturally gravitate towards biblical references of soldiers and warfare. I can easily relate my spiritual and life journey to the concept of battle. We see conflict in: strained relationships, societal tensions, financial pressures, health challenges. And the list goes on. We may even face church disappointments at some point. Often, life feels like a battlefield, with casualties bringing hurt and woundedness.

Our minds, hearts and spirits can be assaulted suddenly with the intensity of a tsunami. The unrelenting persistence is like the never-ending drip of a leaky faucet, wearing us down with a constant stream of challenges. Each injury can affect us spiritually and emotionally (or even manifest physically!). It can be challenging

> **Let the truth of who God says you are affect the way you live.**

during these moments to imagine anything close to what scripture declares us to be:

> *"In all these things we are more than conquerors through him who loved us."*
>
> Romans 8:37 (NIV)

When the battle feels relentless, how do we go from wounded to warrior?

1. *Know and embrace your identity—you are a warrior!* Let the truth of who God says you are affect the way you live.

2. *Have a battle plan.* A battle plan is a strategy used in military engagements to accomplish a goal or tackle a problem. We start the battle on our knees. As we move forward to walk in victory and combat the enemy's attacks, we can use the tools and training that God has given us in His Word.

3. *Celebrate the victories.* Across the world, military victories are celebrated. In fact, some national holidays were created to be a lasting memorial for future generations. These moments happen with others in community, just as soldiers fight together as a team. It's important to take time to recount our own stories with others and give thanks to the Lord for His victories.

> **"But thanks be to God, who always leads us in triumph in Christ, and through us reveals the fragrance of the knowledge of Him in every place."**
> 2 Corinthians 2:14 (NIV)

Life can be hard. We will undoubtedly get hurt and experience pain in our journey—it's proof that the battle is real. Yet be encouraged, friend, you do not fight alone—God is with you.

PROMISE OF HOPE

We are more than conquerors in Christ Jesus.

REFLECTION

What have been your battle victories?

21

The Potter's Wheel

"He said, 'Can I not do with you, Israel, as this potter does?'
declares the Lord. 'Like clay in the hand of the potter, so are
you in my hand, Israel.'"

Jeremiah 18:6 (NIV)

Have you ever watched an experienced potter effortlessly shape a mound of clay into a beautiful vessel? It looks so easy and relaxing initially, doesn't it?

After many years of wanting to try it, I took a pottery wheel workshop with my daughter. My experience working with clay was much harder than how it looked when I first saw it on TV.

On two separate occasions, a piece of stiff clay fell off my unskilled hands as I was trying to mold it. Each time it broke, I had to start the process all over with a new piece of clay. Getting everything to stay centered on the fast-spinning wheel was difficult. But to properly create what I wanted, correct positioning was necessary. The struggle was real!

This experience is much like the way we view other things in life. Scrolling through social media feeds or talking with the people we meet—everything often seems so much easier and better for others. What we attempt doesn't always bring about the same results. More specifically, it doesn't seem as good, beautiful, successful, valuable, or effective, as what others do.

Comparison is a losing game. When we look at images other people are presenting; we are only looking at a highlight reel. We don't see what really goes on behind the scenes.

God made each one of us on purpose, for a purpose. We are unique and loved by Him. We are the work of His masterful hands. There's no need to compare who we are or what we do to other individuals.

There will be times that you may feel off-centered—like a wobbly piece of clay on the spinning wheel of life. But you can focus on staying in the center of the Lord's pottery wheel and let Him continue to mold you to be all that He intended you to be.

Promise of Hope

God will continue to lovingly shape us.

Reflection

How does knowing that you are made on purpose, for a purpose, affect the way you see yourself and respond to others?

22

Once Upon a Time

"**O**nce upon a time..." It's the famous first line of every memorable fairy tale. Storylines often have a challenge weaved in, but eventually end with a passionate love that overcomes all obstacles.

Your story also started out similarly: "Once upon a time, a beautiful baby was born. She had been fearfully and wonderfully created. Her father, the King of Kings, loved her beyond comprehension. He had great plans for her that were filled with hope and a future."

> *"I praise you because I am fearfully and wonderfully made; your works are wonderful, I know that full well... Your eyes saw my unformed body; all the days ordained for me were written in your book before one of them came to be."*
>
> Psalm 139:14,16 (NIV)

Your story may have begun with God's love, but your life may not have turned out to be the fairy tale you had hoped for.

Maybe life has treated you like Cinderella's cruel stepfamily, or maybe Prince Charming never showed up. Regardless of what has taken place in your life already, you have a unique story. Your past, present, and even your future, can be used to inspire others in their journey.

God knows your complete story. Your life had its beginning with Him, and as a believer, when this life ends, you will spend eternity with Him. Everything written on the pages between the beginning and the end of your story is called the messy middle. There could be many plot twists, but be encouraged—your story ultimately has a 'happily ever after' ending.

PROMISE OF HOPE

God knows our story.

REFLECTION

Where are you in your story?

23

Terracotta

S etting out to visit a friend at her new home, I reflected on the name of the town that I was entering into the GPS: Terra Cotta. While most of us associate terracotta with pottery, historically there was a distinction in terms. Terracotta was often the name given to objects not made on a potter's wheel, such as figurines. The type of vessels made on a potter's wheel were called pottery. The material used may have been the same, but the use was different.

God never intends for us to be a figurine merely sitting on a shelf to be admired. We are meant to be a vessel that serves a divine purpose. There are so many similarities between us and this kind of pottery that is formed on the potter's wheel—it's no wonder we are likened to it in scripture. Like the materials in pottery, humanity was formed from the dust of the earth; you could say that Adam was the original "earthenware." However, like pottery, we are fragile and can easily break into many pieces; this damage can be physical, emotional, mental, or spiritual.

> *"Yet you, Lord, are our Father. We are the clay, you are the potter, we are all the work of your hand."*
>
> Isaiah 64:8 (NIV)

We are a vessel hand-crafted by the Lord, the master potter, and formed uniquely for a purpose. We are to carry His light and gospel to the world. What a comfort it is to know that despite our frailty and weakness, God's loving handprints are all over our lives.

Stay yielded on the potter's wheel, where you can continue to be molded into a vessel of unique design and purpose.

Promise of Hope

We are God's workmanship, and He is not done with us yet.

Reflection

How is God continuing to shape you?

24

Born to Reign

I am so thankful that God doesn't judge us like people do. It doesn't matter what we look like, who is in our social network, or what is in our bank account; the Lord sees the treasure and potential that is hidden inside each of us.

When God sent the Prophet Samuel to anoint a new King, neither he nor David's father expected him to be chosen. Samuel initially thought David's eldest brother was the one, but after all seven brothers had passed by, David had to be called in from the field for Samuel to see him. They hadn't even invited David to this special moment!

> *"But the Lord said to Samuel, 'Do not consider his appearance or his height, for I have rejected him. The Lord does not look at the things people look at. People look at the outward appearance, but the Lord looks at the heart.'"*
>
> 1 Samuel 16:7 (NIV)

Not everything spoken over our lives materializes instantly — usually, there's a process. Although David was anointed to be king that day, he would have to hold on to that promise for over a decade before it was fulfilled.

> The Lord sees the treasure and potential that is hidden inside each of us.

Obscurity (The Beginning): David was faithful with the sheep that were entrusted to him. He developed his skills such as fighting, shepherding, and even music in seclusion. It was during this time, with only his family as an audience, that David received his anointing to be king through the prophet Samuel.

Notoriety (The Messy Middle): This was the time of waiting for the promise to be fulfilled. David moved from being a nomadic shepherd to being a nomadic warrior. As he was running from King Saul, he traded leading sheep to leading people as others joined him. Throughout Saul's murderous pursuit of him, David still displayed faithfulness – no longer to sheep, but to God.

Royalty (Achievement): With fulfilling the promise, the title was established. David went from a pasture to a palace; from tending sheep to tending a kingdom; from fighting with a slingshot to fighting with a sword; and from battling animals to battling armies.

Whether you feel hidden or lost in the messy middle, God sees your heart and will fulfill His promises as you continue to be faithful to Him. He has anointed you, so straighten your crown—you were born to reign!

PROMISE OF HOPE

God sees our hearts.

REFLECTION

What phase of life are you in: the beginning, messy middle or place of achievement? What is God seeing in your heart?

25

Qualified to Serve

Is there something that God is calling you to do that you don't feel qualified for? So often we can become preoccupied with our external circumstances, thinking that it is what qualifies us for a role.

We may even try cultivating an impressive image to present to the world. If we don't measure up to a certain standard (ours or others), it's hard to believe God could ever use us in any significant way. Our focus becomes our deficiencies and inadequacies, rather than our surrender to the Lord. If you find yourself in that situation, then draw comfort knowing that you are in good company.

> God has supplied us with everything we need to grow in our faith journey.

Moses was responsible for leading the nation of Israel out of captivity from Egypt. Yet, when he received that directive from God, he disqualified himself:

> **"But Moses said to God, 'Who am I, that I should go to Pharaoh and bring the Israelites out of Egypt.'"**
>
> Exodus 3:11 (NIV)

Gideon led a severely reduced Israelite army victoriously over the attacking and suppressive Midianites, but he didn't see himself as a leader:

> *"'But, Lord," Gideon asked, 'how can I save Israel? My clan is the weakest in Manasseh, and I am the least in my family.'"*
> Judges 6:15 (NIV)

Jeremiah prophesied to the nation of Israel during his time, and his words are still shared thousands of years later, yet he did not think he was a speaker:

> *"'Ah, Sovereign Lord,' I said, 'I do not know how to speak, I am only a child.'"*
> Jeremiah 1:6 (NIV)

When facing insecurity about stepping into something new or bigger, biblical examples remind us that God will equip us. It's unnecessary to gain some type of invisible gold medal or degree for qualification. We simply need to give ourselves to the Lord and follow His leading. If God is asking you to do something, He will help you.

PROMISE OF HOPE

God will equip you to do the work He calls you to do.

REFLECTION

What is God leading you to do?

Hope Unhindered
in Everyday Life

26

Mistakes

> *"When Yahweh delights in how you live your life, he estab-lishes your every step. If they stumble badly they will still survive, for the Lord lifts them up with his hands."*
>
> Psalms 37:23-24 (TPT)

How do you feel when you mess things up? Do you laugh it off and keep moving? Does it make you more determined than ever to succeed? Personally, I hate it. My perfectionist streak causes me to ruminate over the mistakes I've made, making me feel like a failure. Fortunately, there's good news: *failure is not final, and stumbling does not mean stopping.*

Sometimes we focus more on ourselves for the ways we have tripped up, rather than directing our attention to the One who has the power to help us stand tall. At other times we can become consumed with making the right decision for our career or relationships. We become so afraid of making a mistake instead of trusting that the Lord will get us to our destination.

Is there a time and place for righting a wrong we've done? Yes. Will we face a negative consequence of a poor choice that was made? Maybe. But will God abandon His children? NO.

Don't despair when you think that you have messed things up somehow. The above scripture reminds us that God hasn't left us, nor given up on us. He takes pleasure in us, He will guide us, and He will steady us when we falter. You're so much more than your mistakes; you are infinitely LOVED by God!

Promise of Hope

God establishes and steadies our steps – we are in His grip!

Reflection

What is your response to your own mistakes?
Where do you need God's help?

27

Friends

As a child in a military family and as an adult in a pastoral ministry family, I moved around a lot. I've had friends come and go in my life more often than others may experience due to moving around. There's some truth in that old saying, "Distance makes the heart grow fonder or wander." While this statement is likely intended for love interests, the adage applies to friendships too – especially those pre-internet relationships that relied on letter-writing and long-distance phone calls.

Some people have many friends, while others don't. Some friends influence us with positive choices, but others… not so much. Certain friends come into our lives for a season, while others remain for a lifetime. No matter what they look like, we can see the existence of relational bonds everywhere in life.

A beautiful example of friendship in the Bible is the one between David and Jonathan. They fought hard battles together and shared moments of laughter and tears in life's journey. Despite David suffering persecution from Jonathan's father, Saul, the pair remained loyal to each other until the end.

We are made for community. In fact, even the most introverted person still needs a friend. Of course, finding and keeping good friends can be a challenge.

"...but there is a friend who sticks closer than a brother."

Proverbs 18:24 (NIV)

Life can feel lonely without someone to vent your frustrations to, pour your heart out to in a time of debilitating grief, or alternately, when you want someone to celebrate exciting moments with. In those times of feeling alone, remember God is there with you. He is listening and interested in your life—God is your closest friend.

PROMISE OF HOPE

We are never truly alone. God is with us.

REFLECTION

What does your friendship with God look like?

28

No Pain, No Gain

U ndoubtedly, you've heard the expression, "No pain, no gain." If you've ever begun a workout regime, you know that within a couple of days of that initial session there's definitely a degree of pain involved. Those muscles are not accustomed to being used like that, but with repetition, they'll strengthen and increase in size.

When it comes to working out, athletes know the importance of stretching their muscles. Sometimes it can feel uncomfortable, but it's important to prevent injury to our bodies.

The act of stretching also relates to our walk with the Lord. No matter what area of our lives is being stretched, the process does NOT feel comfortable at all. However, this action causes us to become more flexible, stronger, and healthier. Our reach grows and we are capable of more.

The prophet Isaiah gave the Israelites hope-filled instructions during a painful time in their history. When these directives were applied, God's people would experience increase after their captivity.

> *"Enlarge the place of your tent, <u>stretch</u> your tent curtains wide, do not hold back; lengthen your cords, strengthen your stakes. For you will spread out to the right and to the left..."*
> Isaiah 54:2–3a (NIV)

There it is again—the stretching. Amid their painful circumstances, God's people needed to stretch and expand. Whatever 'tent' we are in, wherever God has placed us, it's time to stretch and expand our reach. Do what feels uncomfortable, and you'll get stronger. Take bold strides forward to what is waiting for you. Don't shy away from the pain—there's so much more for you to gain!

Promise of Hope

Stretching will bring strength and expansion.

Reflection

In what ways might God be asking you to stretch?

_____

_____

_____

_____

_____

_____

_____

_____

_____

_____

_____

_____

_____

_____

_____

_____

_____

_____

_____

_____

_____

_____

_____

_____

_____

_____

_____

_____

29

Perfect Example

B efore a play-wrestling match or tickle fight with my young kids, I used to joke around by trying to muster my best 'tough guy' impression. Standing tall, I would puff out my chest and raise my arms. Then, in the deepest voice possible, I would utter this iconic challenge: "You wanna piece of me?" At the moment that I spoke, everyone would smile, knowing fun was about to ensue.

It didn't take long for my kids to start imitating me. At random times, when they wanted to play with me, they would stick out their chest, wave their arms, and repeat the same challenge. Somehow, my daughter, Lauren, misunderstood what I had been saying. For the longest time she would loudly ask, "You wanna piece of MEAT?" Perhaps, I needed to articulate better, because without clarity there is confusion. Of course, over time, Lauren learned what to say after paying closer attention to my words.

Children tend to emulate what they see. This may be why the apostle Paul referred to believers as children and instructed us to follow God's loving example:

> *"Follow God's example, therefore, as dearly loved children and walk in the way of love, just as Christ loved us and gave himself up for us as a fragrant offering and sacrifice to God."*
>
> Ephesians 5:1-2 (NIV)

Jesus' life was a perfect example for us on how to live. He came to this earth and offered His whole self for us, not just a 'piece' of Himself. Even though He had power and authority, He didn't take on a 'tough guy' persona. He loved sinners—people who didn't always understand or get things right. Then, in an act of selfless love, He died for all of us. His death won the ultimate battle over sin and the grave.

Like the people in the stories of Jesus, we all make mistakes, yet He still loves us. As we navigate life, we can look to God's Word to learn from Jesus how to live.

Promise of Hope

Jesus loves us and provides a perfect example of how to live.

Reflection

How can you follow Jesus' example and walk in the way of love with others?

30

Overflowing

I have a white ceramic canister set sitting on my counter. It's pretty, but even the largest one is not big enough to hold the contents of a new bag of sugar. When it is time for a refill, I will start pouring the sugar and then stop periodically to shake the container to help settle its contents. I will keep pouring and shaking until the sugar starts to spill over the top. The vessel may be full, yet I have more to give.

This visual makes me think of many of us, as we give of ourselves to help others in different ways. There is a promise that, as we share our resources, finances or time, the Lord gives generously back to us. Although the way God blesses us back may take a different form than how we initially gave, no matter how much we give, we will always end up with an excess. This is God's kingdom economics.

Not only does scripture show the principle of sowing and reaping, it also demonstrates that there will be an overflow in what the Lord gives us:

> *"Give, and it will be given to you. A good measure, pressed down, shaken together and running over, will be poured into your lap. For with the measure you use, it will be measured to you."*
>
> Luke 6:38 (NIV)

The last line in this verse carries a challenge for us. We are to examine our own giving when feeling like we are living with a deficit: **"*For with the measure you use, it will be measured to you.*"**

Like the jar of sugar on the counter, there might be times in our lives where we feel empty and need to be refilled. Thankfully, we're not meant to stay that way. The Lord has much more to give us. As He pours out His blessings, He will fill us to overflowing.

Promise of Hope

God blesses those who give.

Reflection

In what areas of your life are you giving?

31

Distractions

M y loyal dog loves summer days laying on the patio. He peacefully and calmly surveys our yard until that moment when he inevitably notices a squirrel. All his attention then shifts to that little creature, and he pays little mind to my voice. Like my canine companion, we can get sidetracked by what's presently going on around us or with thoughts of future scenarios. As the distractions pile up, they can become an interference that prevents us from being able to listen to what the Holy Spirit is trying to say.

It's often been said, "Don't let the noise of the world keep you from hearing the voice of the Lord." While that's great advice, it can be challenging at times. So, what are we supposed to do when so much is competing for our attention, tempting us to become overwhelmed? Scripture tells us:

> *"Christ's resurrection is your resurrection too. This is why we are to yearn for all that is above, for that's where Christ sits enthroned at the place of all power, honor, and authority! Yes, feast on all the treasures of the heavenly realm and fill your thoughts with heavenly realities, and not with the distractions of the natural realm."*
>
> Colossians 3:1-2 (TPT)

Instead of allowing things to distract or weigh us down, we must intentionally go after the things of God that deserve our attention. This isn't to say that we should never think about earthly things, but rather be mindful of how much of, and to what things we give our attention to.

The Lord has so much more for you and me than what the world tries to interest us in. When we fix our minds on things above, we can have better clarity in seeing things down here from God's perspective and in hearing what He wants to say to us.

Promise of Hope

God has so many better things to set our minds on that can fill us with hope.

Reflection

What has been distracting you lately? What might the Holy Spirit be wanting to speak to you about?

_____

_____

_____

_____

_____

_____

_____

_____

_____

_____

_____

_____

_____

_____

_____

_____

_____

_____

_____

_____

_____

_____

_____

_____

_____

_____

_____

32

Cruising

One thing I enjoy most about going on a cruise is the delicious and plentiful food. With so many tasty options nearby to choose from, I can have a meal or snack almost anytime I want—my stomach never growls. As someone who doesn't enjoy cooking very much anymore, I love that I don't have to prepare the food and I don't have to clean up afterwards either. I simply show up when I want to eat and leave when I am finished. Win-win.

Of course, normal everyday life doesn't exactly work that way—at least not for me. My fridge may not always be full, but even with many choices, my children still complain that they're hungry because supposedly there's nothing to eat! More often than I care to admit, I fall into the same habit of opening the doors of the fridge and pantry to look inside. I close them quickly after coming to a similar conclusion as my kids – there's nothing to eat.

For several reasons, the perceived needs of our stomachs may not be met, and we're left feeling starved and longing to be filled. Of course, our hunger and thirst can extend far beyond just food and drink. So often we look to things or people around us to fill the empty areas in our lives but remain unsatisfied.

"Then Jesus declared, 'I am the bread of life. Whoever comes to me will never go hungry, and whoever believes in me will never be thirsty.'"

John 6:35 (NIV)

There's nothing in this world that's been able to completely meet all my emotional needs—and nothing that could ever meet my spiritual needs—but God. In the moments that I feel depleted and empty, I turn to the Lord to fill me up as only He can do. Like my cruise ship dining experience, staying close to the Lord as my source is what allows me to be continually nourished by Him.

Promise of Hope

God alone can satisfy our souls.

Reflection

What are the areas in your life in which you are feeling a hunger and a thirst for something that only God can satisfy?

33

Transforming the Shadows

L et me start by saying that I do love the colour gray—a lot! However, after having a dark gray colour adorn the walls of the main living areas in my house for far too many years, I needed a drastic change. It was time for the gray to go away by replacing it with something that would make my space feel light and airy. I even viewed the paint switch, in part, as a symbolic act of faith to let go of past things, and to embrace the bright newness of what the future held. The colour I chose: Alabaster White.

The dark shadows in my home disappeared. Although nothing else seemed to change in my life right away, my mood elevates every time I look at the transformed space. What a difference paint can make, altering the feel and look of everything around it.

In a more powerful way than a colour change, God's light transforms everything.

> *"When Jesus spoke again to the people, he said, "I am the light of the world. Whoever follows me will never walk in darkness, but will have the light of life."*
>
> John 8:12 (NIV)

We're not meant to walk in darkness—not the darkness of sin, or the dark pall that can be cast over our lives from the challenges and cares of this world. Instead, we're meant to walk in God's light.

Perhaps the darkness in this life has been casting its shadows on you; affecting your moods and actions lately. Fortunately, it's unnecessary to undertake a project as labour-intensive as painting a house to have more light. There may be practical or symbolic steps that we can take as we continue to follow Jesus and wait for deeper change to come in our lives. It is time for the gray to go away!

PROMISE OF HOPE

God's light illuminates our path.

REFLECTION

What do you need to let go of from the past? What do you need to embrace to experience more of God's light in your life?

_____
_____
_____
_____
_____
_____
_____
_____
_____
_____
_____
_____
_____
_____
_____
_____
_____
_____
_____
_____
_____
_____
_____
_____
_____
_____
_____
_____

34

Faith Plan

There are times in life that I like to keep my options open and make decisions in the moment based on how I feel, such as choosing a restaurant when I am hungry. I don't want to commit myself to eating sushi, if when the time rolls around to eat, I would rather have tacos instead. Regrettably, I tend to be a commitment-phobe when deciding on restaurants in advance.

However, when it comes to trying to achieve something that is particularly important to me, I usually prefer to have a step-by-step plan. I want a system or procedure to follow that will help move me towards my objective.

In our faith journey, when the aim is to experience Jesus more fully and express this knowledge in our life, having a plan helps us get closer to that goal. The qualities listed in scripture give us clear steps that we can take to help us achieve the results we are pursuing.

"His divine power has given us everything we need for a godly life through our knowledge of him who called us by his own glory and goodness ... For this very reason, make every effort to add to your faith <u>goodness</u>;
and to goodness, <u>knowledge</u>;
and to knowledge, <u>self-control</u>;
and to self-control, <u>perseverance</u>;
and to perseverance, <u>godliness</u>;
and to godliness<u>, mutual affection</u>;

and to mutual affection, <u>love.</u>
For if you possess these qualities in increasing measure,
they will keep you from being ineffective and unproductive
in your knowledge of our Lord Jesus Christ."

2 Peter 1:3,5-8 (NIV)

Sometimes we can second-guess ourselves. We wonder if we are doing the right things and start to question how much we are moving forward in our walk with the Lord. Be encouraged friend, we have hope because God has supplied us with everything we need to grow in our faith journey. He has even given us a plan that we can follow. Continue to practice the steps needed to add to your faith. In doing so, you will not only grow in your knowledge of God, but you will also produce spiritual fruit.

PROMISE OF HOPE

God has given us everything we need for a godly life.

REFLECTION

What are the areas that you are growing in? Are there any steps that you
are struggling with?

35

Scavenger Hunt

H ow are you at navigating scavenger hunts? I'm not great at solving riddles or figuring out maps, but it all makes sense once I reach the destination. They say hindsight is 20/20, and most times I would agree with that statement.

When the Israelites left their bondage in Egypt, they found themselves trapped at the edge of the Red Sea. With Pharaoh's army pursuing them, they were unable to flee any further. The Lord had directed Moses where to lead the people, but now they were caught between a sea and an army. The directions didn't make sense to them—surely someone misread the 'map'!

> *"As Pharaoh approached, the Israelites looked up, and there were the Egyptians, marching after them. They were terrified and cried out to the Lord. They said to Moses, 'Was it because there were no graves in Egypt that you brought us to the desert to die? What have you done to us by bringing us out of Egypt? Didn't we say to you in Egypt, 'Leave us alone; let us serve the Egyptians'? It would have been better for us to serve the Egyptians than to die in the desert!'"*
> Exodus 14:10-12 (NIV)

God had a plan to show his might and faithfulness to bring the Israelites to their promised land. We know how the story ends, but they

> When God parted the waters, the barrier became the bridge and eliminated the opposition.

did not. This seemingly impossible situation wasn't a surprise that God had to reconfigure.

As believers, we may not always understand why God is leading us in a certain direction or why we are in a specific situation. The clues on our own life's scavenger map may not always make sense. At times, we may question our position, much like the Israelites did before God made a way for them. When God parted the waters to walk through, not only did the barrier become the bridge to freedom, it also eliminated the opposition.

"Moses answered the people, 'Do not be afraid. Stand firm and you will see the deliverance the Lord will bring you today. The Egyptians you see today you will never see again. The Lord will fight for you; you need only to be still.'"

Exodus 14:13-14 (NIV)

This same God that delivered the Israelites is the same God who will deliver you.

PROMISE OF HOPE

God is our deliverer.

REFLECTION

What are the places of impossibility in your life where you need God to make a way for you?

36

Wait to Move

This is a fast-paced world. We are equipped with thousands of devices to help us increase our efficiency and get more things accomplished in less time. Yet, we are often left drained in our quest to push ahead with commitments and responsibilities.

It is important for us to remember that to move forward in God's strength, there is waiting before there is movement. We need to take time to stop before we can go, rather than go until we are forced to stop.

> *"He gives strength to the weary and increases the power of the weak. Even youths grow tired and weary, and young men stumble and fall; but those who hope in the LORD will renew their strength. They will soar on wings like eagles; they will run and not grow weary, they will walk and not be faint."*
>
> Isaiah 40:29-31 (NIV)

When we take the time to wait on the Lord, He will give us the power and ability to:

Fly like an eagle. Soaring in the sky enables us to see the big picture. Because of the change in perspective, things that once seemed large and daunting, now become small. Just as eagles will fly above the clouds to avoid rainfall, when you face rain clouds of adversity, you will be able to rise above them.

Run our race. God's strength helps us to keep going. Running implies moving quickly—we will be effective in accomplishing what needs to be done.

Walk through life. We will keep moving and not give up. Walking is moving at a thoughtful pace. This speed allows us to see more clearly what is happening around us, as well as to appreciate seeing things up close at a more relaxed stride.

The common thread in all these things is: movement. The key to accomplishing this is spending time with the Lord, waiting expectantly for His divine gift of strength. The Lord is waiting for you with open arms, inviting you to rest in His presence to gain strength to move.

PROMISE OF HOPE

God will give us the strength to keep moving forward.

REFLECTION

How is your time spent waiting on God affecting your movement?

37

Work Weary

O ne night, I was watching an online video with my son Nathan, who was still young at the time. Nodding towards the worship band singing on the screen, I jokingly asked, "When you're on the stage one day, will I get to go see you for free or will I have to buy a ticket?" Immediately, in all seriousness, he responded with, "Nobody will have to pay, because I'll be sharing the gospel and that's free for everybody." I had expected him to laugh and say, "Of course not mom!", so I felt a bit embarrassed at my silly question. It was encouraging, though, that he already knew this important truth at his young age – the Good News of salvation that Jesus offers is a gift for us all.

For various reasons, I still sometimes find myself acting in ways that seem as if I'm trying to earn God's free gift. This is like buying a ticket to see my own son on stage instead of enjoying the perks of being his mom. Neither actions are necessary. We live in a society where money and achievement are prioritized over relationships. This environment makes changing our mindset a challenge when it comes to accepting God's free gifts to us.

"Stop *striving* and know that I am God..."

Psalm 46:10 (NASB)

Thankfully, our position as God's child is not based on endless attempts to earn his love, but rather, on the single decision to accept his gift of life. You may be weary from trying to prove your worth or striving to earn God's acceptance. Friend, give yourself permission to stop and embrace the fact that you are already His beloved child.

PROMISE OF HOPE

Salvation is God's gift of love to us.

REFLECTION

What have you been trying to earn, that God already said is yours?

38

A Dark Night

A n anti-government sentiment was held by a fracturing nation. This attitude was fueled by four competing sects vying for power to lead the dissatisfied Jewish people. A mandate was imposed by the oppressive government ruling the land. As a result, many individuals, like Mary and Joseph, were temporarily separated from their families. Fulfilling this requirement brought about financial cost and great inconvenience to people.

It was a dark time for the Jewish people when Jesus was born, both politically and spiritually. For four centuries God had not spoken to His people. It was also a dark night for the shepherds in the field when the angels appeared and announced Jesus' birth. In that pivotal moment, heaven shattered the silence, and the light of hope pierced the darkness.

> *"An angel of the Lord appeared to them, and the glory of the Lord shone around them, and they were terrified. But the angel said to them, "Do not be afraid. I bring you good news that will cause great joy for all the people."*
>
> Luke 2:9-10 (NIV)

The appearance of an angel can be a terrifying thing. Perhaps, this explains why so often in scripture, angels would begin their message to people by saying, "Do not be afraid." I love how God initially had only one angel appear to the shepherds to break the ice before having a multitude of them show up afterward. Despite such an overwhelming encounter, the angel's instructions were followed.

The shepherds sought out The Good Shepherd, and after finding the baby Jesus, these men set out to tell others about the hope that they had found. Later in this chapter, the shepherds were found praising and glorifying God, much like the angels had been doing earlier in this passage.

> **Don't be afraid, your Saviour has come to bring your heart peace and joy.**

Like the shepherds, we can also go through dark periods in our lives. The unrelenting darkness and stifling silence fill our existence as our prayers seem to go unheard.

Friend, may the Lord's message bring you hope. Don't be afraid; your Saviour has come to bring your heart peace and joy. As you continue to seek Him, may your wanderings and wonderings be transformed into fulfilled promises and praise.

PROMISE OF HOPE

God brings light and hope into our darkness.

REFLECTION

What are the wanderings and wonderings in your life? How have you experienced God's light and hope in your life?

39

The Way of Love

While taking a seminary course, I studied the early church and its comparison to the western one of today. I learned how those believers transformed their society through their conduct. Turning from pagan practices to following Jesus' example for living distinguished these individuals. Most notably, it included loving their enemies unto death. The early church was defined by their love for others, even those that hated and persecuted them. It's difficult to imagine such extreme love displayed in the face of so much torture and abuse.

Newsreels today are full of fighting and victimization. Though to lesser degrees, conflict even happens amongst Christians, unfortunately. This world needs change, and the early church has historically proven that we can and are to be the change.

Imprisoned in Rome, the apostle Paul penned the following words for the church in Ephesus, a large city that was a center for pagan worship:

> *"As a prisoner for the Lord, then, I urge you to live a life worthy of the calling you have received. Be completely humble and gentle; be patient, bearing with one another in love. Make every effort to keep the unity of the Spirit through the bond of peace."*
>
> Ephesians 4:1-3 (NIV)

It amazes me that, despite the injustices that Paul faced, he still chose the way of love and encouraged others to do the same. This scripture pushes me to go against my natural emotions and society's damaging messages to live in a way that reflects God's love. In doing so, we play a role in bringing change to our world.

Promise of Hope

God can help us change the world as we walk in the way of love.

Reflection

What changes might God be challenging you to make to better live out Ephesians 4:1-3?

40

Share Your Story

On my office desk sits a little black wooden sign that I received as a Christmas gift. In bold white text, it says, "A good friend knows all your stories, a best friend helps you write them." This delightful present also included helpful supplies for writing. It was a thoughtful gift from a special friend to inspire me towards my writing goals.

When I think about how the message on this tabletop decoration relates to me, I am also reminded of Jesus. He is the best friend who knows each one of our stories in detail, and He helps us share our stories of Him with others.

> *"That which was from the beginning, which we have heard, which we have seen with our eyes, which we have looked at and our hands have touched—this we proclaim concerning the Word of life... We proclaim to you what we have seen and heard, so that you also may have fellowship with us. And our fellowship is with the Father and with his Son, Jesus Christ. We write this to make our joy complete."*
>
> 1 John 1:1,3-4 (NIV)

John was one of the three disciples that Jesus kept closest to Him. He was even referred to as "the disciple whom Jesus loved." He enjoyed a close relationship with Jesus and others might have even ascribed 'best friends' status to their relationship.

Scholars believe that the apostle John authored the book of 1 John while he was in exile on the island of Patmos. He wrote from his encounters with Jesus, so that others could also experience the life that God offers them. Although John's movements were restricted in exile, he continued to impact the world by sharing his testimony through writing. There was still a story in his situation.

Like John, we all have a story to tell. While our circumstances may vary, and the medium that is used can differ, the message of God's plan of salvation remains the same. There's still a story in *your* situation that is waiting for you to share.

PROMISE OF HOPE

God knows us, and He has given each of us a story to tell.

REFLECTION

What is the story of your relationship with God? How, and with whom, can you share it with?

Did this book encourage you in a special way?
Your feedback helps other readers like you discover meaningful books. It would mean the world to me if you took 2 minutes to share your thoughts about this book as a review. You can leave a review on the retailer of your choice and/or send me an email with your genuine feedback.
lifeunhindered.ca/review

Acknowledgements

I want to thank the Lord for the hope that He gives and for His faithfulness that has brought me to this point in my life.

To my family and the many friends who have cheered me on in this writing journey, it's your encouragement that has given me the fuel to keep going.

To my husband Hansley, thank you for giving me the space I needed to create and for helping me launch this book.

To my parents, Paulette and Yvon, you have always believed in me and cheered me on to greater things.

To Tammy, Tamara, Shawna, and Mary, thank you for the unique ways each of you have nurtured this project.

To my beta readers: Emily, Val, Stephanie, and Jen, your feedback and investment of time in the editing process has been a vital contribution.

To Emily Grabatin, thank you for your effective coaching, guidance, and attention to detail. You have helped me successfully navigate this publishing journey. I truly appreciate all that you have done for me.

To the incredible Fight4Freedom staff, you planted the seed to publish these writings. In doing so, you unknowingly became the original beta readers for much of this book.

To Shelley, my amazing college roommate from many years ago. Thank you for sharing your love of devotional books with me. You always managed to find inspiring passages to read together that would touch my heart. Those encouraging messages taught me that it only

takes a few hope-filled words to make a meaningful impact in someone's life.

About the Author

GINETTE ARMOOGAN is passionate about people finding and living in freedom. She enjoys helping others discover who they were created to be and encouraging them to live out their life purpose. Ginette loves bringing hope, healing and help to people. With 30 years of pastoral experience, she serves as an ordained minister, certified life coach, social justice advocate for individuals impacted by exploitation and trafficking, and lover of all things beautiful.

Ginette lives in the Greater Toronto Area with her husband and three children. She delights in deep conversations and bubble tea.

To learn more about Ginette, you can connect with her:

Website: LifeUnhindered.ca

Email: ginette@LifeUnhindered.ca

Ginette Armoogan
Transformational Coach
www.LifeUnhindered.ca

MOVING FORWARD IN FREEDOM

The following resources are available to assist you in your move from weariness towards well-being:

~ Join the free 5 Day **Healthy Habits Challenge** to strengthen your mind, soul and body. These quick and easy action steps can help bring refreshment to your life.

~ Download 24 free scriptural **Affirmations for the Weary**. Find encouragement as you declare the truth and hope that God brings.

~ Journey with me to unlock your dreams and unblock your path through **Transformational Life Coaching**. Take your first step today!

Visit www.Life.Unhindered.ca to access all these supports and more!

36290552R00105